YOUTHS

EMPOWERED FOR SUCCESS

TAKE THE RIGHT ACTION TODAY FOR YOUR SUCCESS TOMORROW

Terrence Fagan Jr.

15-Years-Old

Copyright © 2019 by Terrence Fagan Jr.
ISBN 978-1-7338585-0-2
All rights reserved.

Publisher's Cataloging-in-Publication Data provided by Five Rainbows
Cataloging Services

Names: Fagan Jr., Terrence, author.
Title: Youths empowered for success : take the right action today for your
success tomorrow / Terrence Fagan Jr.
Description: Covington, GA : TFJ Group, 2019. | Series: Youths empowered
for success.
Identifiers: LCCN 2019903174 | ISBN 978-1-7338585-0-2 (paperback)
| ISBN 978-1-7338585-1-9 (ebook)
Subjects: LCSH: Youth--Life skills guides. | Youth--Conduct of life.
| Teenagers--Conduct of life. | Success. | Inspiration. | Achievement motivation
in youth. | BISAC: YOUNG ADULT
NONFICTION / Inspirational & Personal Growth. | SELF-HELP / Personal
Growth / Success.
Classification: LCC HQ796. F34 2019 (print) | LCC HQ796 (ebook) |
DDC 305.23--dc23.

Published by: TFJ Group LLC,
170 Cinnamon Oak Cir., Covington, Georgia, USA

Library of Congress Control Number: 2019903174

For information about special discount on bulk purchases, please make contact at
Terrence@YouthEmpowermentPodcast.com

This book is dedicated to youths! Remember that no matter where you are from or your circumstances, you possess the innate ability to be great. Your circumstances should not define you, instead, be motivated by them.

WHAT YOUTHS AND EDUCATORS ARE SAYING ABOUT TERRENCE FAGAN JR. AND HIS BOOK "YOUTHS EMPOWERED FOR SUCCESS"

Terrence has always demonstrated leadership qualities and a concern in the way youths behave. Therefore, it's not a surprise that he has written and dedicated a book to his peers. Terrence wants to see youths demonstrate their true potential now.

Jada Pearce
10th Grade High School Student

I'm impressed that at 15 years old, Terrence sees the need to inspire and empower youths through social media, his Youth Empowerment Podcast and now through his book Youths Empowered For Success. Terrence is an inspiring mentor.

Khalif Timmons
11th Grade High School Student

It is such an awesome feeling to see my own peer doing what he has been doing to motivate us as youths to be the best version of ourselves now. Terrence's book is a must read for us youths.

Blair Alston
11th Grade High School Student

I'm impressed to see an inspirational book dedicated to youths written by a youth. This is an indication of the future we'll have. For a 15-year-old to dedicate so much of his time to empower his peers to the extent of writing a book to help them, he's seriously on a mission. Do what you can to help this young man further his mission. Go get a copy of Youths Empowered For Success.

Reinhard Davis
Educator for over 20 years

OTHER PUBLICATIONS FROM TERRENCE FAGAN JR.

1. My Daily Action Planner
2. The Prayer Journal
3. My Thankfulness & Gratitude Journal

CONTENTS

ACKNOWLEDGMENTS

I have so many persons to say thank you to! You have all played different but significant roles in my life for which I am grateful.

First, I want to say thank you to God for making everything possible. To my dear dad Terrence who ensures I have a balanced life, words cannot explain what you truly mean to me, you are my hero and I love you dearly. To my mom and coach Sophia I say thank you for exposing me to the things regular youths are not exposed to. You push me beyond my limits and for that I'm thankful. You tell me every single day how possible my dreams are and to be focused on them. To my big sister Shanique who thinks she's my mom, thank you for the support, the tough love and the examples you have set for me to follow, I love you. To my grandmas Beverly, Cynthia, my granddad, my aunts, uncles, cousins and other siblings thank you.

To my editor Shanique Miller, thank you for a job well done. To my past and present athletic coaches Mr. Corey Bennett, Mr. Foster thank you. Thank you, Mr. Bennett, for instilling in me very early the importance of believing in myself. To my teachers from past and present schools, Hydel Preparatory, Jamaica, Ms. Zahra at Maddoc Elementary, Sir John A McDonald, Canada; Conyers Middle school, Rockdale High and my current school Newton High USA.

To Mr. Mike Schryer who wrote the foreword for my book thank you. I will always remember those empowering talks you gave me the first time I met you in Toronto at that self-development conference when I was just 12 years old.

To my church family at Brampton Deliverance Ministries Canada and Voices of Praise and Newton Baptist Church, USA thank you for your love and the spiritual guidance!

Last but by no means the least, if you have inspired or helped me in any way and I've failed to mention you by name it's not intentional. Thank you so much.

FOREWORD

Terrence is a natural born leader you can learn from!

I first met Terrence as a 12-year-old when he attended a powerful self-development conference in Toronto and again when he attended my Facebook Mastery training workshops. I'm inspired, that at only 15 years old, Terrence not only invests in his education by attending personal growth seminars and workshops but is now sharing his wisdom as the Author of his first book: "Youths Empowered For Success: Take The Right Action Today For Your Success Tomorrow".

Terrence guides his peers, pre-teens and teens alike, to make better decisions and take the right action to ensure a better future for themselves, their families as well as society in general. As a passionate young leader, Terrence is leading his generation to be the change the world is looking for to ensure a better world for all of us to live in. You'll want to follow Terrence because he is using his amazing social media channels to get his inspirational messages out to the world. He is also the author of numerous journals which are currently sold on Amazon.

Attention Parents! Terrence has dedicated one whole chapter to you! Children must receive the love and support they need from their Parents. So, learn from Terrence to set up your children for success and a life of happiness.

Whether you are a pre-teen, teen, young adult or a parent, this book is a must read! Get ready to be inspired while empowering youths to take the right action today for the success they want tomorrow.

Mike Schryer
CEO iInspire Inc.

ABOUT THE AUTHOR

Terrence Fagan Jr. is a 15-year-old youth mentor. He's the founder and host of Youth Empowerment Podcast. A show which inspires, empowers and give business ideas to youths through captivating real-life stories of youths who are experiencing success and experts from varying industries. His show is aired on Apple Podcast (iTunes), Google Play Music, Spotify and Stitcher Radio. Terrence is an online entrepreneur.

Terrence is simultaneously enrolled in college and high school. By the time he graduates high school, he'll graduate from college with an Associate of Science degree in Computer Programming.

He is the author of numerous journals which are currently sold on Amazon. They are My Daily Action Planner; My Thankfulness & Gratitude Journal and The Prayer Journal.

Terrence is a member of his school's track and field team. He's a fitness fanatic who enjoys working out.

Terrence is on a mission to inspire and empower his peers to take the right actions today to ensure they have the success they want for tomorrow.

To support Terrence on his mission of youth empowerment via his show, Youth Empowerment Podcast, visit **www.YouthEmpowermentPodcast.com** go to the subscribe page to subscribe; download and give a 5-start rating and review. Connect with Terrence on social media **@TerrenceFaganJr**. and **@YouthEmpowermentPodcast**. To get free youth mentorship, simple join his new Facebook group "Youth Empowered For Success".

To contact Terrence for Speaking Engagements, Interviews and/or Youth Mentorship please do so by visiting **www.YouthEmpowermentPodcast.com** or email **Terrence@YouthEmpowermentPodcast.com**

TO MY READERS

My book will provide you with a message of inspiration, empowerment and transformation. You see, age is just a number and you are never too young to start charting a deliberate path to your success.

In fact, I have shared some of my own experiences and successes in this book, not to boast, but to show you that everything is possible if you believe you can and take action.

The earlier you start taking the right action to chart your success path, the earlier you will experience success.

Like many persons, you'll experience failures; when you do, learn from them and continue to take deliberate and consistent action. Remember, the key to achieving any goal is consistency, a positive mindset, action and connecting with the right people. Youths Empowered for Success inspires you to do that so much more.

As you go through the pages of my book, just know that you were born to succeed. No matter what your circumstances are or where you are from, everything is possible if you want them to be.

Be ready to be inspired and empowered as I share very important factors to being successful as a youth. Always remember this, never stop believing in yourself and your abilities to make your dreams your reality.

THE AIM OF THIS BOOK

This book is aimed at empowering and inspiring other youths to take the right actions now for the success they want tomorrow. It provides valuable tips youths can use to help them to demonstrate their true potential whilst still enjoying their youthful years.

If you are a parent, this book is for you too. I have outlined in an entire chapter some of the things we want from you our parents. Often times, our parents are not clear on what exactly we want from them and therefore they are not able to totally give us that.

I decided to share my thoughts with my peers because it might help them to better understand knowing that it is coming from one of their own. I have decided to write this book because too many of my peers are doing so many things which they are taking them on a path of self-destruction. Truth is, there is another way and we must find it and live.

There is a better path! A path which takes you to happiness, fulfilment, joy and success. Can you get there following the masses; deliberately absenting yourself from school; drinking excessively; engaging in nefarious activities?

No, you will not!

You have to change your thinking, your habits and your connection with a deliberate intent of doing things differently.

TO WHOM THIS BOOK IS FOR

This book is for you if you are a pre-teen, a teen, parent, guardian or anyone who has youths under their control. It is aimed at speaking directly to youths from the perspective of one of their peers.

Youths Empowered For Success will inspire and empower youths to dream big and believe themselves. They will be reminded of the power of the mind and the importance of taking action now to achieve the success they desire. Youths who read this book are getting it from the perspective of one of their peers which is powerful.

I have seen youths around me doing both the good and things which need to be changed. And guess what, if you are doing things which people classify as bad, it's not you. It's the choices you make, the attitude you have and the actions you take.

You can improve all of that. You just have to be intentional about improving yourself. As I move to chapter 1 of this book, I say to you, "look within yourself today and make the effort to change at least one thing which you know needs to be improved."

INTRODUCTION

Now more than ever youths need to be empowered, inspired and affirmed for them to take action to demonstrate their true potential.

We are living in a time where technology has advanced so much that everything is just a mouse click away.

Whether for the good or the bad, you are more exposed than ever before. This is so for youths especially, as we are naturally curious and want to experiment.

The fact is, yes you are more exposed to negative influences via the internet. However, the opportunities which now exist on the internet are endless.

You can use the same internet to learn so many different things to improve your knowledge base.

Be focused on the things which will move you forward in a positive way. Be curious about things that when you learn them, they edify you and build you up.

My friend, your mind is so powerful that when you use it to your advantage and take action, sky is the limit for you. Well, let me tweak that slightly. When you have a positive mindset and you take action, you are your limit. Meaning, put no limit on your potential, because you can be and do anything you want to be.

You just need to have big dreams, believe in your abilities to make those dreams your reality and take action. Take small action steps even when your circumstances are not what you want them to be.

We are living in a time where parents, guardians and other caregivers need to be more equipped with parenting skills. They not only need to be equipped with parenting strategies but effective parenting strategies which will ensure they are at their best for their children to be at their best too.

As I write the pages of this book and think about me being 15 years old and the millions of other teens out there, I often times wonder, "why are so many youths on a path of self-destruction."

And the truth is, they are capable of being anything they want to be. They can do so much more than they are now doing.

Come on youths, wake up and embrace your awesomeness and your greatness. Believe in yourself. Believe in your abilities to do great things

Too many youths are associated with friends who are heading nowhere. It's a harsh statement to make but that's the reality for many. Look around you and see for yourself. Most times friends do similar things and even if it isn't so, that is what is assumed by others.

My peers take it from me a 15-year-old, you don't need to be associated with individuals who are not able to add value to your life.

No matter your age, you can say no and don't feel bad when you actually do.

Don't feel bad when you have to say no to people who are on a path of self-destruction. You don't need to be associated with them out of pity. If you really want to help those youths who are not doing right for themselves and others, report it to a responsible adult who has the capacity to help them. Remember you are pretty young and trying to find your own, so don't allow yourself to be bugged down with other people's problems.

Whether you are at school or anywhere else, assess individuals by observing what they do and say. For example, when you are at school, look at the students who are always in trouble with the teacher.

Whether they're in trouble for disruptive behavior, not turning in assignments on time, chatting a lot in class which usually cause disruption or always absent from class! You don't need to be friends with those students. You are not obligated to.

You don't need to say or do things to fit in. You are already a great person with big potential. Always remember that you are here for a purpose and you should not let anyone divert you from that.

Think of your end results all the time. Ask yourself this question, "do those the friends I have share my goals and dreams?"

Based on your evaluation of those students, your answer should be a definite yes or no. If its yes, of course they can be your friends. However, if it's no, keep them at a distance.

As you read through the pages of this book be inspired and empowered to start taking action now. Not tomorrow, next week or even next month, start taking action now. Remembering that, your tomorrow starts today.

SECTION 1

YOUR MIND IS POWERFUL SO GIVE FOCUS TO WHAT YOU THINK ABOUT

Growing up, there's one very important thing that my mom constantly spoke to me about. She would say, "Terrence J, you can achieve anything you want to achieve. Dream big, and never stop thinking about what you want until you achieve it." Yes, I did take action too.

Today, I can tell you that her talks are not in vain. I did exactly that even when things seem to be going wrong. I kept my mind focus on the things I want, and they are becoming my reality. You too can do the same and in this section of my book, I'll help you to do just that.

CHAPTER 1
FOCUS ON YOUR GOALS NOT YOUR CIRCUMSTANCES

CHAPTER 1.1
YOU WERE BORN SPECIAL

What sets you apart can sometimes feel like a burden and it's not. And A lot of the time, it's what makes you great.

-Emma Stone

Youths!
It is not very easy to see yourself as being special. Especially when you are not hearing it from the people, you love the most. It is really awesome to hear my parents, my teacher, family friends, or my church family affirm me by telling me that I am special.

However, the fact is, you will not hear those

affirmations all the time. Always remember, you are special whether someone says it to you or not. You must believe it and take the necessary step to be it.

When you believe that about yourself, no matter what negative words people might say to you or about you, it will not affect you so much. Why? Because you already know that you are special and no one else can tell you otherwise.

Being special means there is nobody else out there in the world like you. Yes, you are absolutely special. You were born for a purpose and with time you will know what that is. You are beautiful human being. Let no one tells you otherwise.

Affirm yourself every time you get the chance to do so. Affirm a family member, a friend or a classmate. You might not know how much you have made their day when you do that.

On the following page, make a list of five (5) unique characteristics about yourself. Simply write 5 things which make you special.

Your Task:

Make a list of 5 Things Which Make You Special.

1.

2.

3.

4.

5.

6.

7.

8.

9.

10.

Terrence Fagan Jr.

CHAPTER 1.2
YOU ARE NOT YOUR CIRCUMSTANCES

Your circumstances should not define you. Focus on the solutions not the situations.

What do you see when you look in the mirror? Do you see an individual who is special, smart and has the ability to achieve anything he/she wants to achieve?

Yes, you are absolutely correct if you are looking at that individual. You are all of those and more.

In fact, no matter what your circumstances were or still is, you should not be defined by them. No, you are not defined by them unless you allow them to.

Your circumstances should motivate you to dream big. They should propel action which will ensure those big dreams become your reality.

You can achieve anything you want to achieve if you let yourself. You have to first start believing that everything is possible and start taking action to make it happen.

Think about what you deem as a negative situation as the opportunity to learn something which will guide you through life. Tell yourself that you will learn something new every day, even what other see as negative.

In fact, your circumstances should definitely guide your future actions, based on what you have learnt from your past experiences.

I know situations are not easily erased but that's not the point. The point is, you are bigger and bolder than your circumstances. That is, if you let yourself!

Whether it's the exam you have failed. The separation of your parents which you blame yourself for. Your family's inability to provide you with the things you think you need. A mistake you have made like teenage pregnancy or the smoking habit you have picked up.

Others make you feel like the nobody. You are more than all of those. Yes, you can overcome all of your mistakes, failures, challenges, setbacks or obstacles. You have to believe you can and take the necessary action to make it happen.

Sometimes you are not able to see it, but there is always a positive in what seems like a negative situation.

Let's look at the example of your parents got divorced. I know it's your harsh reality. But chances are you are now going to get everything double.

In the past, mom and dad would buy you one gift of behalf of both of them. Now, mom will buy you her own gift and dad will do the same. I will take it a bit further by saying they will want to outdo each other with whom can buy the bigger and more expensive gift.

Whatever it is for you, just know that your future is not a representative of your past. It is you demonstrating to yourself that you can be anything you want to bc.

Your Task:

What are two lessons you can learn from a situation you have experienced which you have deemed bad?

1.

2.

CHAPTER 1.3
YOU BECOME WHAT YOU THINK

*The things you think about the most will
manifest itself in your life.*

-Sophia Davis-Fagan

Have you ever thought about how powerful your mind is? If you are like me in my early years, you probably have never given serious thought to the power your mind holds.

I'm just a 15-year-old and yet I have started to see my goals manifesting in my life as I give focus to them and take intentional action.

You see, you can start to experience happiness, joy and success no matter how young or old you are. You have to first believe that it can happen and take the necessary to ensure it does. Believe without a doubt that you can achieve anything you set your mind to.

As young as you are, you can start place yourself in the successes you want to achieve in your life. For example, say you want to attend one of the top universities in your country with a full scholarship. Start with the expectation of receiving your acceptance letter.

As a matter of fact, you can start seeing yourself already at the university. Get photos of your university and place in your room or anywhere you are able to see them constantly. As often as is possible, think about it and see it no other way.

Have you gotten a clear picture of what I'm saying yet? All I am saying is this: you become what you think about every single day. So, you must be conscious about the things you give focus to.

You might be saying that is sounds hard right now, but as you grow from your youthful years into adulthood, you will realize that it becomes even more difficult.

Simply put, the earlier you start training your mind to give your dominant thought to the things you want in your life and not the opposite, the sooner you will achieve them.

Meaning, do not give focus to the things you don't want in your life. Example, you want the A grades in your exams, don't think about what if you failed. Instead, start thinking about the A grade you will get and take action to make it happen. Yes, make sure you study and be fully prepared to get the A grades you so desire.

My mom would tell me, "Terrence J, wanting something and thinking about it every day will not give it to you unless you take action to get it." So, I'm telling you now, have those big dreams; think about them constantly and do all you can to make them your reality.

When the doubts and negative thoughts go in your mind, stop immediately and turn them into positive statements of the things you want to achieve.

The things you think about the most will manifest itself in your life no matter how young or old you are.

On the following task page, make a list of two short term goals you want to achieve and at least one action you will take to make it happen.

Your Task:

Make a list of 2 short term goals you want to achieve and at least one action step to get you on the path to making them happen. Example, you need to get a mentor to guide you on your career path.

Cons #	2 Short Term Goals	Action Plan
1		
2		

CHAPTER 1.4
GIVE YOURSELF POSITIVE SELF-TALK

*One cannot be prepared for something
while secretly believing it will not
happen.*

-Nelson Mandela

How often do you do self-talk? The fact is, we all do self-talk every single day, whether it is positive or negative. The truth is, for many persons, negative self-talk is the dominant self-talk they have.

As a youth, it's the best time for you to start practicing positive self-talk. Why? Like with everything else, this is no different. The more you practice positive self-talk the more it will become a part of what you do. It helps you to discard the negativity and embrace more positivity.

The domino effect is that it has significant benefits for you. The things you tell yourself has a lot to do with the actions you talk. By extension, your actions will determine the success you have or the lack thereof. Just know that you are not too young to start thinking about the kind of life you want to have.

You see, for you to experience success later, you must start taking deliberate and consistent action now. This is coming from your own peer, a 15-year-old youth who is practicing this. If I can do this, I know you can too do it too.

Get in the habit of start practicing positive self-talk and try to be consistent with it.

Like I said earlier, you will definitely become what you think about the most, so you must be conscious about the self-talk you have.

Remember, your self-talk is the thoughts you have every day. I will reinforce this by saying that you are not too young to be deliberate about the thoughts you have.

Be consistent with the positive self-talk and work on getting rid of the negative self-talk you have. Negative self-talk does not serve you and will never either. If nothing else, negative self-talk brings negative things in your life. It makes you fearful, doubtful with little no belief in yourself.

To encourage positive self-talk, you have to start affirming yourself. Make affirmation statements about the goals you want to achieve. Whether those goals are immediate like passing mid-term exams or long term like buying your first car or house.

Your consistent positive self-talks will propel you to take action which will get you on a path to achieving your goals.

Do you want to connect with self-motivated youths who are success driven and, on a path, to achieving great things? Simply ask to join my Facebook group Youth Empowered For success.

As you create your affirmation statements, make sure you write them and say them as often as possible. Make a vision board with images of the goals you want to achieve. View them as often as possible and make a mental picture of you occupying them until they become your reality. Tell yourself every single day that those goals are yours to achieve.

Youth Empowerment Podcast & Youth Empowered For Success Facebook Group

I am the founder and host of **Youth Empowerment Podcast.** A show which is dedicated to inspire, empower and give business ideas to youths through captivating interviews of real life stories of youths who are succeeding and valuable tips and strategies from expert. To subscribe and download episodes go to: **www.YouthEmpowermentPodcast.com**

My Facebook group **Youth Empowered For Success** I just created to help you to be among other youths who are serious about achieving greater success. Simply ask to join: **Youth Empowered For Success** on Facebook.

CHAPTER 1.5
SAVE OUR GENERATION FROM SUICIDE

Your life has value so never believe anything else.

We all can agree that suicide has become a menace to our generation. Should it continue to be so? Let's all say no in unison.

So many youths have taken their own lives and left their loved one in sadness and disbelief.

They often time wonder what they did wrong and what could they have done differently.

It is too late for those who have gone already but there's still time to save many youths who struggle every single day for varying reasons.

Now that you and I have agreed that suicide will no longer plague us. Let me ask you this, "how often have you felt like the world is against you and nobody really cares"? That feeling of being boxed in a corner with no way out!

Guess what, you are not alone. So many youths have those feelings due to their situations and circumstances.

But when your mind begins to tell you that nobody cares, that's an outright lie! There is no truth to it.

Most times those feelings come about when you think you are just not in control. You do have control even though it does not feel like that.

In fact, those thoughts and feelings are lies which your mind tells you as a result of what you feed your mind with.

Take it from me your peer, a 15-year-old who has experienced struggles just like you! There are many persons who actually care for you and really want to help you.

Think about three persons in your life right now who love you unconditionally and would do anything for you. Go share your thoughts and feelings with one of them right now.

You might be right; the world might not care because they don't know you! But the people who matter the most do care, and they love you because there's just one you. Your parents, your friends, your teachers your neighbors those are just few of the persons who are cheering for you.

One very important thing I want to tell you right now – LOVE YOURSELF. Love yourself like there's no love for anyone else. Show yourself love every day. Look in the mirror and see how wonderful you are.

Let me remind you that as individuals, it's normal to have struggles! Don't keep your struggles to yourself. Share it with your loved ones. Let your family members, a trusted adult or even a friend know what you're going through!

Tell it all. Don't hold it back. The earlier your start sharing your thoughts and feelings with your loved ones, the better they'll be able to help you as you help yourself.

In fact, the more you open up and share those feelings the better you'll feel! Whether you are sharing with a trusted person or you are making notes in your diary, share it. Don't internalize it. You're freeing your mind of the negative thoughts and feelings to open up a whole new world of possibilities.

My peers, there's always a solution to every issue you're going through. Even when it seems there's none; look at the bigger picture! Your life forms part of that solution. Love it! Cherish it! Save it! Don't take your life!

Think positively despite the negative feelings you are having. Make sure you surround yourself with uplifting individuals both physically and virtually. People who inspire, empower and motivate you to be your best even in the midst of your struggles. This makes a big difference.

Feel free to come on and be inspired by the free value I share to inspire teens on social media @terrencefaganjr and on my podcast Youth Empowerment Podcast. I just created a Facebook group just to inspire and empower youths like myself. Search for "Youths Empowered For Success".

You see, you might not be able to come up with solutions to the struggles you're faced with, but others can, and they will. Give them the opportunity to help you! Just share your thoughts and feelings with them.

And you're still not comfortable talking to your loved ones, there are people at the National Suicide Prevention Lifeline rooting for you! Just call or text them at 1800-273-8255!

For persons who observe that your friends or loved ones are not acting how they would normally act, don't wait! Talk to them or alert someone who is capable of providing support to them.

Let's start looking out more for the youths around us. If this allows us to save at least one life, I'm sure it would have been worth it.

You're preventing the pain associated with suicide in a home, which could be your own, a community and by extension our society! Let's get to work.

Terrence Fagan Jr.

CHAPTER 2

VIRTUES TO HELP YOU ACHIEVE

CHAPTER 2.1
BE SELF-MOTIVATED

There are no secrets to success. It is the result or preparation, hard work, and learning from failure.

-Colin Powell

Are you a self-motivated individual? Did you answer yes? That's great if you are self-motivated. You get things done without the motivation of others.

Well, if you are not, it is the perfect time to start building your self-motivation. Being a youth, you have the advantage of easily learn and adapt more easily than if you were older.

A self-motivated individual is more like to be more propelled to take action to achieve greater success than others who depend on others to motivate them.

You see, self-motivation will give you the drive and a sense of urgency to do those things which are important to achieve your goals. It definitely puts you in urgency mode and lets you do what needs to be done to achieve your goals.

Self-motivation makes you more committed to not only your personal goals but for others as well. When you are driven by self-motivation, you never sit and wait on others to get you to take action. You know somethings need to be done and you will get them done in a timely manner. You will have no excuse not to get your tasks done because you know the importance of the outcomes.

Being a self-motivated individual makes you more confident, organized and helps you to manage your time more efficiently.

Generally speaking, motivation pushes people to take action. However, when you are motivated by self, it moves beyond just wanting to achieve to a personal drive to do what's necessary to ensure you achieve your goals.

Your drive to achieve greater success even at such a young age means you are committed. A commitment to capitalizing on the opportunities which come your way and a willingness to learn from the mistakes and failures you've experienced. Are you self-motivated?

On the following page make a list of five or more things which motivate you.

Your Task:

Make a list of 5 or more things which motivate you.

1.

2.

3.

4.

5.

6.

7.

8.

9.

10.

CHAPTER 2.2
BE FOCUSED NO MATTER WHAT'S HAPPENING AROUND YOU

*Focus on where you want to go, not on
what you fear.*

-Tony Robbins

Remaining focused on the important things is one of the hardest things to do no matter your age. Now more than ever, the distractions out there can be so irresistible.

For us youths, it is very easy to be distracted from the things which will ensure that we enjoy our youthful years whilst still remaining focused on the things which are important to create a bright future for us.

Sometimes even the pressures of being perfect at home at school and at church can be distracting in itself.

Why? Because, you are caught up doing the things which seek to please everyone.

Can you please everyone? No! Don't even make attempts to do that. Instead, with the help of the people who wants the best for you, look at the important things and give focus to those.

If you are serious about giving focus to the things and people who will help you to achieve your goals, then be committed. Your commitment will drive you to succeed no matter your age.

Have you started to see the importance of being focused yet? Remember, not just been focused but to be focused on the things which will move you forward in a positive way.

Some Of The Distractions

The internet is one the most distracting things. With the advent of social media, more youths are even more distracted.

They spend far less time focusing on the important things. Instead, most of the day is spend scrolling through social media.

I can tell you as a teen myself, it is very tempting. Social media will consume you if you allow it. Have control and remain focused.

To be honest with you, it can be very distracting. However, I'm blessed to have parents who are serious about keeping me focused. I am constantly reminded on a daily basis about this. So even if I wanted to allow the internet to consume me, I am just not allowed to do this.

Everything is about balance, and my mom would tell me, "Terrence J if the scale is going to be tipped, it should be more towards the things which will benefit you." Needless to say, she is serious about this.

Like my parents remind me, I'm taking this opportunity to remind that you are to keep your focus no matter your circumstances.

Whether or not you have your parents to help you to keep your focus, you can do it. Your future is dependent on you, so don't let yourself down. The actions you take now, will determine the kind of future you will have.

Guess what, remaining focused even as a youth is very important. It is just never too early to start remaining focused.

For us as youths, its remaining focus to

ensure we do great in elementary/primary school, high school and college or university attend.

I'm sure like me, you have big dreams even at your age. The best way to ensure you get to your goals is by focusing on the things which will help you to achieve them.

My friends, another distraction is the playing of the different games we love so much. Whether it's the X-Box, the PS4 or just finding the internet games to play, they can be very distracting sometimes.

Remember, you have to enjoy your youthful years because it only comes once. However, don't allow it to take away from your homework or study times and even family time.

The business you want to start might just be idea away even at your age. Everything is possible if you are intentional about the things that you do now.

Keep your focus; in time as you get older, you will see the importance of it.

One way of keeping focus is to do a weekly schedule and stick to it. Take a little time to do your schedule. If you cannot do a weekly one start with the daily schedule. I have done one for you on the following page; you just need to fill it in.

Your Task: Make your schedule here.

Weekly schedule for (your name)							
Time	Mon	Tue	Wed	Thu	Fri	Sat	Sun
6:30 – 7:30							
7:30 - 8:30							
8:30 - 9:30							
9:30 - 10:30							
10:30- 11:30							
11:30- 12:30							
12:30 - 1:30							
1:30 – 2:30							
2:30 – 3:30							
3:30 – 4:30							
4:30 – 5:30							
5:30 – 6:30							
6:30 – 7:30							
7:30 – 8:30							
8:30 - 9:30							
9:30 – 10:30							

CHAPTER 2.3
RESPECT GOES A LONG WAY

*When you respect others, it goes right
back to you.*

Whether you are a preteen, a teen like me
or even a young adult respect definitely
goes a far way.

The more you respect others, the more they
will respect you. As you get to your teen, it's a
time where your body goes through lots of
changes. If you are not careful, you become the
teen nobody recognizes.

Why? Because of those changes some teens
sometime get angry easily to the point of being
disrespectful to people around them.

This is not the right thing to do at all. When

you have issues with others, you should make the effort to talk it through in a respectful way rather than using disrespectful language to deal with it.

You can control your emotions and you should.

Practicing this from this early age will instill in you value. Morals and values which will take you through life.

You will have respect for self as you do others. Not only that, but you will start learning to respect authority.

Can you imagine all of us as youths start demonstrating this kind of behavior?

I have heard this said so many times before that kids are the future. Can you image the change starts with us as youths? Think of it seriously, what would our futures look like?

For me, I see a world where people start dealing with conflicts better. A society with more love and less crime and violence. How about you, what kind of world do see with the change starts with each of us youths?

On the following page, write down at least two things you can change about yourself which will effect the kind of change you want to see in others.

Your Task:

Write down at least two things you can change about yourself which will effect the kind of change you want to see in others.

1.

2.

3.

4.

5.

6.

7.

8

9.

10.

CHAPTER 2.4
HONESTY STILL COUNTS

Be honest in your doing, because when
trust is broken it's hard to be
regained.

Being honest as a youth is not always the easiest thing to do. However, it is something which if practice will become a part of who you are. You will be honest at all times even if it means being unpopular. So even at our age, we have to make the decision to be honest no matter what.

I have always been told by my mom that everything in life has options even when it appears that there is none. So, let this be one of the things you intentionally do because in the long run you will benefit from this.

My parents have always said that I must be honest with them no matter what the situation is. Because this is the only way they will be able to really help me if God forbid something goes wrong.

Honesty is very important. If you fail to be honest, what you are essentially doing is setting yourself up for a negative outcome. When people find out you are not an honest person, it's the hardest thing to change. If you look at the individuals who tell lies, they have to consistently use one lie to cover the other. The individuals who steal, most times move on to something bigger each time.

Don't let this be you. We all are born with the natural tendency to be and do good. Overtime those dishonest behaviors are learnt. I implore you that you should not allow yourself to be known for being dishonest. It's hard to reverse.

As a youth, you might have observed what many youths do to fit in with their peers. Some of them do crazy things to include dishonest behaviors.

Personally, I don't believe that we should have to do this to fit in. As youths, we have to learn to accept each other no matter where we are from so there will no need to be dishonest to fit in with our friends.

On the other hand, our parents should instil in us the importance of accepting ourselves for who we are. If this is taught to us from home, then we will not have the need to lie to fit in. If your peers are not able to accept you for who you are then they are not worthy to be your friends.

I will share with you an example of when parents instil good values in their kids how hard it is for them to depart from it. This is about my own sister who is 13 years older than I am! I heard it from my mom. My sister Shanique came home with a little swelling on her face, our mom asked what had happened and she told her that kids were fighting, and she had to separate them, and, in the process, she got hit. Needless to say, my mom was not happy at all.

They went to bed. Late in the night my mom heard a sobbing which turned out to be my sister. She went to my mom's room sobbing because she lied, and she knew the importance of being honest and the consequence of lying. She told my mom the truth about how she got the swollen face. My mom wasn't pleased; however, she was happy that at least she went and did the right thing by correcting the lie she had told earlier.

The moral of that story is that when children are taught the right values at home, they will not stray too far from them. Sometimes when they do, they come back eventually. I encourage you that if you ever give an inaccurate story, the right thing to do is to go back and correct it. Be honest no matter what! Honesty still counts.

CHAPTER 2.5
BE RESPONSIBLE

*The more responsible you are, the
more forward moving you become.*

How responsible are you as a pre-teen or
teen? To be responsible at this age is not
the easiest thing to do. This is the time when
you want to have friends. You want to be
playing your video games for hours. You want
to surf the internet and all the other things
which your age group wants to be involved in.
I am sure you understand where I'm coming
from.

My peers, we are pretty young, and we want
to enjoy our youthful years. However, we still
can be responsible and doing some of the

things that we love to do. Just remember moderation is important. You should balance things by ensuring you get things done which will move you closer towards your goals whilst doing the things you love to do.

My parents have always said that it does takes a lot to be responsible at our age. The fact is, you can be responsible no matter your age. You have to be intentional about it. The earlier you start trying to be responsible, the more it will be engrained in you to be.

Simple things like keeping your room neat and tidy. That is being responsible. Your parents should not have to clean your room for you. These are simple but very important things that will help you to get in the habit of being responsible.

Another task which you must do to be responsible as a youth is to focus on your school work. When you get homework, your parents should not have to constantly ask if there's homework for you to do it neither should the teacher. The responsible thing to do is to do the homework. This is a very important responsibility which you should take seriously.

In addition, be responsible enough that if you are not able to do your homework or any tasks given, you ask for help in advance. Your parents and teachers are always more than happy to help because they want you to succeed.

As youths, we are born in a time where we are accustomed to nothing else but technology. Everything is easier and quicker to be done. We have access to information more than our parents ever did. However, we are most times not using this to our benefit. Rather than sitting and playing computer games for hours, take a break for a thirty-minute walk. You can even access an exercise program and follow what they do to keep your body fit and healthy. Be responsible with everything you do.

I am sure like my parents, you must have heard it from your parents even once that you need to give the game a break and go get some physical activities done. This is important as it keeps your bodies in shape. So many kids are getting sicknesses like diabetes which were once for the older people. This is as a result of lack of physical activities.

You might be seen as being different when you do the responsible things which are not usually done by many who are within your age group. In fact, it is ok to be different when you are doing the right things.

You don't need to feel uncomfortable with yourself. Instead, be proud of who you are and what you are doing. Talk with your friends and try to get them to do the responsible things as well. They will be glad they did in the long run.

SECTION 2

SURROUND YOURSELF WITH INDIVIDUALS WHO CAN HELP TO MOVE YOUR GOALS FORWARD

I have always been told that the individuals I hang around will determine how successful I become. Upon hearing this and observed it for myself, that statement is always top of mind when I'm selecting my friends.

I suggest you do the same if you are serious about achieving your goals.

CHAPTER 3

HAVE SUPPORTIVE PEOPLE AROUND YOU

CHAPTER 3.1
BE SELECTIVE WITH YOUR FRIENDS

The person who encourages you in your failing times will most likely be there for your successes.

Friendship and friends mean a lot to us as youths. I am sure my pre-teen and teen friends know what I'm talking about.

As youths, we tend to pull away from our parents and draw closer to our friends. This can be a good thing and the reverse is also true.

Good in the sense that we are learning to be

less dependent on our parents and trying to hold our own. However, this can be a detrimental scenario because as you pull away from your parents, you might pull close to friends who share totally different values that you do.

This does not mean you have a disdain for values other people share. Instead, it could mean that the path they are on is not one that leads them forward in a positive way. Those friends might not be the right friends to hang out with.

They might think it's ok to skip classes, they might think it's ok to lie and they might think it's cool to disrespect and disobey authority.

Whether it's their parents, teachers or just about anyone who gets in their way, they just like to defy orders.

Peers who do those things you really don't want them to be your friends. It's just the sad reality. You should respect everyone, but you need to select friends who share your values.

These friends should be honest, respectful, responsible and have great interest in the things which will uplift themselves and the youths around them.

When you do find your friends, your parents

should know them, and their parents know you. You should also ensure that your parents know your friends' parents too. Some of the indicators of who are the kinds of friends you want to hang out with are:

- The students who are respectful to both teachers and their peers.
- Students who are always prepared for class.
- Students who are always early for class.
- Students who engage the teacher, yourself or other students on issues which are motivating and empowering
- Students who usually have their homework ready to submit when it's due.

Some of the indicators of peers you do not want to hang out with are simply the opposite of those mentioned above:

- Students who are disrespectful to their teachers and their peers.
- Students who are seldom prepared for class.
- Students who are always late for class.
- Students who never have their homework on the due date.

- Students who never take responsibility for their own action.
- Students who always blame others for things which happen to them.
- Student who engages others in lude arguments

Your friends have the ability to help to keep you focused and they also have the ability to distract you from the things which are important to create your success. Always remember, be the kind of friend you want from others. Select your friends wisely.

How do you select your friends? On the following page make a list of at least five things you look for in your friends.

Your Task:

Make a list of at least five things you look for in your friends.

1.

2.

3.

4.

5.

6.

7.

8.

9.

10

CHAPTER 3.2
TAKE ADVICE FROM THE RIGHT INDIVIDUALS

*The person who gives you advice must
be capable of providing such advice.*

Who are you taking advice from? Are these persons responsible enough and have the ideal answers to your questions? Well, everyone usually has something to say about everything, even when they are not equipped with the right information you should be getting.

I will tell you this, which my parents tell me all the time. Ask the right persons a question and you will be given the right response. However, if you ask the wrong persons the same question, you will be given the wrong response too. The truth is, sometimes you will not even know that the response is not the ideal one.

The first place you should be looking for answers is from people who are responsible and are capable of providing the correct responses. Your parents mean you well and they will ensure you get the appropriate responses to your questions.

If they don't know, they should be able to get the right answers for you. Your parents are most times your biggest cheerleaders and they want you to be in the know, so go get it from them first.

The other responsible persons you could get your answers from are your teachers, guidance counsellors, mentors and other responsible persons. They have the knowledge because they are trained and have the experience to deal with you.

You could also get the advice from your pastor if you are a youth who goes to church.

For me, I am comfortable asking my church family for advice because I know they mean me well.

Make sure the people you seek advice from

are capable of providing the appropriate answers for you.

The last persons you want to take advice from are your friends. Your friends might know just a little more or less than you know, so getting advice from them would not be a good idea.

The responses you get; if you were to act on them might put you in serious trouble.

Again, get advice from the right persons who mean you well and the persons who come to my mind first are my parents, teachers, pastors and other responsible adults.

Who do you take advice from?

CHAPTER 3.3
GET A MENTOR TO GUIDE YOU
---

*Your mentor must have demonstrated
the ability to direct your path.*

Having a mentor as a youth comes with many benefits. As youths, you are able to call on this person for support and guidance as you go through the different stages of life.

Some of the benefits also include building healthy relationship whilst learning to trust; keeps you accountable and responsible; and it gives you confidence whilst building your self-esteem.

A mentor is that person who you build a relationship with. This person helps to guide you and keeps you on a path which ensures your success. The relationship you build with this person is of such that you are able to call on them to help you deal with some of the issues which pre-teens and teens go through.

In building this relationship with your mentor, you are learning to trust others whilst you are allowing another person to trust you too. Trust is one of those values which is very important in many things that we do now and will do in the future. So, it is very important that trust is taken seriously.

Getting a mentor keeps you accountable and responsible. You meet with your mentor whether virtually or in person and you both have discussion on the things you need to do.

Your mentor might give you a task to do and to report to them at a particular time. You as the mentee will do everything it takes to ensure you get the tasks done, especially if you know your mentor is a no-nonsense person who wants no excuse.

By being punctual when you are to meet your mentor and do all the tasks which you both agreed on actually builds a sense of responsibility and accountability. These are great benefits as they will help you to become the kind of person you, your family and loved ones will be proud of. This will help you to be more successful in high school, college, university, work or entrepreneurship.

The fact that this person is outside of your immediate family and they believe in you it lets you believe that you can do a whole lot. You develop the confidence you need to build your self-esteem. It helps you to confide in your mentor, especially for you if you're the pre-teen or teen who refrain from confiding in your parents anymore.

This person can now serve as your confidant rather than having one of your peers who most times will not give you the right guidance. Have you seen the benefits of your mentor yet?

This person is always affirming you make you feel special. Your mentor constantly tells you that you can do anything you set your mind to; you only need to follow the advice of the people who means you well.

They keep you accountable and constantly guides you in the right path. This definitely builds you up as a person and you realize you don't need to do the wrong things to fit in. Your mentor can definitely help you through those youthful years. In fact, this is the time you need a great support system around you so capitalize on all the benefits of having a mentor.

A quick advice before I close this chapter. If you are not able to get a physical mentor, you can use social media under the guidance of your parents in a way which benefits you. All I am saying is that, you can find persons who are inspiring and empowering, who you could connect with on social media.

They can become your mentor without them even knowing. This is a great way of using social media rather than using it to do the things which have no benefits to you.

On the following page, write down the names of persons you will contact to be your mentor and the persons you will start following on social media for daily inspiration and empowerment.

Your Task:

Write down the names of persons you will contact to be your mentor and the persons you will start following on social media for daily inspiration and empowerment.

Cons #	Names of person who could be your mentor	Names of Persons you could connect with (Virtual Mentors)
1		
2		
3		
4		
5		
6		
7		
8		

CHAPTER 3.4
GET INVOLVED WITH
PRODUCTIVE ACTIVITIES

*The activities you are involved with
should be meaningful.*

Get involved in extracurricular activities at school, church and other community programs.

As a pre-teen or teen, it is very important that you get involved in extracurricular activities. They keep you focused on the things which will move you forward.

There are many benefits to be had from getting involved in the various activities and clubs which your schools and churches offer. Some of these are responsibility, commitment, time management and connects you to new people in addition to exposing you to new things.

It also keeps you occupied so that you won't have the time to get involved in the things you are not supposed to be doing.

Another important benefit that my parents told me about is that it looks good on your application for college or university. People want to see you involve in things outside of your normal activities.

It is important though that you have a balance and get involved in the activities which will not clash with your normal school schedule and not too many which will take you away too much from your school work. Remember, you first priority is your school work

The soft skills you learn when you get involved are priceless. These values are important and will benefit you even more when you get older and you are either working for yourself or working for a company.

Another very important skill which is learnt by being a part of those activities is time management. Your activity starts at a particular time and you want to show up early rather than showing up a bit late. It tells something about who you are and what you are becoming. It is so very important to always be on time. This can be the difference between your success and failure.

An example, you have an exam that might not be your best subject and you get to the exam 5 minutes late. You could have used those 5 minutes to do some more writing to maximize your chance of getting a good grade.

As a pre-teen or teen, you want to develop those habits that will build your character in a positive way.

When you develop great skills and values at an early age, you are planning your success rather than leaving it to chances! The skills you learn so early can turn into something massive later. Don't take it lightly.

On the following page make a list of at least three extracurricular activities you can sign up for now or the upcoming school year.

Your Task:

Make a list of at least three extracurricular activities you can sign up for now or the upcoming school year.

Cons #	List some extracurricular activities you can sign up for
1	
2	
3	
4	
5	

CHAPTER 4

APPRECIATE YOUR CHEERLEADERS

CHAPTER 4.1
SHOW GRATITUDE TO YOUR PARENTS

---

*Honor your father and your mother,
so that you may live long in the land
the Lord your God gives you.*

Exodus 20:12

Do you show appreciation to your parents? How do you normally show them appreciation? So many children give little attention to it, but you need to show gratitude to your parents regularly for what they are doing for you.

Despite the fact that they are responsible for you and are obligated to provide for your basic needs, many go far beyond providing the basic needs and make sure you have all the things which make you comfortable and happy.

Can I name some of the extras for you? The vacations, the gadgets like the games, iPad or the tablet and the list go on.

For me, I'm forever grateful and blessed to have the parent I have. I cannot thank them enough. They have exposed me to the things which many youths my age are not exposed to.

They've provided me with the tools I need to make my mission that much easier to accomplish. That is, to provide my peers with the inspiration and empowerment needed for them to take the right action now to ensure they have a better future.

Don't wait on special holidays like Mother's and Father's Day to make your parents feel special. The least you can do is show them your love and appreciation with even a note or hugs. They cost nothing!

On the other hand, you can save your money and get them a card or little gift or even just to say the words, "I love and appreciate you for what you are doing for me."

In fact, most parents do not require a lot from you. So many of them just want you to be opened and honest with them. They want you to remain focused on the things which will move you forward. Can you start giving your parents that?

Starting today, let us start showing our parents love and appreciation. Go sit and have a talk with your parents.

Tell them how much you love and appreciate them right now. Surprise your parents with a note, letter or a poem. You might just make their day!

Your Task:

Make a list of some of the things you can do for your parents today to show them love and appreciation.

cons #	List some things you can do today to show love and appreciation to your parents
1	
2	
3	
4	
5	
6	
7	
8	
9	
10	

CHAPTER 4.2
BE COOPERATIVE WITH YOUR TEACHERS

*As a student, when you take
responsibility for your learning, you
get more out of your teachers and you
learn more.*

As youths, it is very important that we play our part to cooperate with our teachers to get the most out of our teachers. This is one of the ways to get full benefit of your learning experience.

It makes it easier not only for the teacher to teach you but for you to learn in an environment which is not regularly affected by disruptive behaviors.

Your teachers are not your parents.

However, they are fully responsible for you when you are at school. They know what they are doing because they are trained to do so.

Take responsible for your learning and don't add to their stress. I mean stress in the sense that teachers work so hard to ensure our success, yet they are paid so little.

When you take responsibility for your learning, it will enable you to learn more and achieve more in the long term.

If you should ever have an issue with your teacher, be respectful in trying to resolve it. If that does not work, the best way to deal with it is to ask for excuse from the class and go to your school counsellor or your principal.

This way, you will not be disrespectful to your teacher and you will not disrupt the class and prevent your fellow classmates from learning.

Always remember too, be open with your parents and talk with them about the things which happen at school.

What this does not only for you but for your classmates is showing that there is a right way of resolving conflicts. You are showing others that when you communicate in a respectful manner, conflicts can be resolved.

Disrespect and disruption only make a situation get worse and that should not be your aim. When you cooperate with your teachers it creates a better learning environment not only for you but for the other students.

On the following page write at least three things you can do to cooperate with your teacher and three things you can do to take responsibility for your learning.

Your Task:

Write at least three things you can do to cooperate with your teacher and three things you can do to take responsibility for your learning.

Cons #	3 things you can do to cooperate with your teachers.	3 things you can do to take responsibility for your learning.
1	Submit my homework on time	I'll ask for help if I don't understand a topic.
2		
3		
4		
5		

CHAPTER 5
YOU ARE THE LEADER WHO TAKES ACTION

CHAPTER 5.1
BE THE LEADER YOU ARE

*As you wake up each day, always
aim to be the kind of person others
want to emulate.*

To be a leader as a youth is not as difficult as you think it is. Yes, we all know the power of peer pressure. But you can start by being yourself.

You are innately a great person, you just need to acknowledge it, believe it and make the effort to demonstrate it.

However, you have to always remember that

you will not be able to fit in all the time especially if you are one of those youths who does the right things most or all of the time.

Some of the self-development books that I have read state clearly that there are skills and values which are practiced by great leaders.

They postulate that if you become aware of them and decide to start building and instilling them in myself, you too can be a leader even as a teen.

Some of these are managing your time well; having a positive mindset no matter what's happening around you; associating with the right people, a never giving up attitude and so many more.

I am sharing this with you because we are all capable of doing anything we want to do. Yes, you are capable of being anything we want to be once we set our minds to it.

Are you willing to try to do the right things all the time even if you do not have friends because of that?

You have to be willing to do this. It will be worth it. In the long run, your peers and people in general will respect you even more because they realize that you stand for something.

Some of your peers will actually start

following what you because they now observe the result of your action. This is exactly what you want to happen. You must be leading by good example.

Despite the fact that you want to be a leader, you have to also be a follower of people who are displaying great examples. This will add to the standards you set for yourself and strengthen the values you are already holding.

CHAPTER 5.2
TAKE STRATEGIC ACTION EARLY

The actions you take today will
determine the success you'll have
tomorrow.

The perfect time to start taking action is now. No matter your age, today is the time to move. Procrastination is never a good thing. It delays your success. Why delay the things you can do today for another day.

As a youth, age is your advantage. Start taking action now when you have little to no responsibilities. The older you become, the more responsibility you have.

Taking action for you can mean just getting information about things you want to be involved in. A very important one for me is the Dual Enrolment program.

Sometime after I started attending high school, I heard about this program and decided I would get more information. It turned out that once you are in high school you be enrolled in college and high school simultaneously for free or at a reduced cost.

You can guest the action I took. I did get enrolled. Therefore, by the time I graduate high school, I well also graduate college with an Associate of Science degree in Computer Programming.

If you are in the United States and attending high school, I encourage you to take advantage of that opportunity.

This puts you ahead of the pack. It definitely gives you the advantage. For example, when you are trying to get into university, you will have the edge over other applicants.

There are so many other opportunities you can take action to capitalize on. Another one is the notes you have been making in your diary or gadget. You can turn those notes into a published book.

Just by becoming a published author, you have now opened a whole new world of opportunity for yourself. You can make a business out of writing just one book.

All the opportunities I'm directing you to, I have been utilizing myself. I have taken action and they are working for me.

At only 15 years old, I have written numerous journals, hosting my own show, 'Youth Empowerment Podcast' and now publishing this book to inspire my peers.

The fact is, you can take action to do the same and so much more. You are your only limit. You possess an innate ability to be great.

Believe in your abilities; dream big; set realistic goals; have a positive mindset and take action to make those big dreams your reality.

Remember, the deliberate actions you take today will enhance your chances of achieving success tomorrow.

On the following page make a list of at least 3 action steps you can take now to improve yourself. (you can take your fist action by creating a daily, weekly or monthly action plan)

Your Task:

Make a list of at least 3 action steps you can take now to improve yourself.

1.

2.

3.

4.

5.

6.

7.

8.

9.

10.

CHAPTER 5.3
RESIST PEER PRESSURE

*You are courageous! You can truly be
who you are and be happy.*

I am sure you have been in a situation where you've been pressured to do things which you are not supposed to do.

If not yet, I can assure you that you will encounter at least one peer pressure situation as a youth. Guess what, you don't have to fall prey to peer pressure!

You are stronger than you think you are, and you possess the strength within to resist peer pressure.

Remember, you are a leader in your own right and you don't need to follow your peers to fit in. If you have to follow your peers, always follow those who display behaviors which will help you to succeed.

Peer pressure can be powerful and very hard to resist. However, you should always remember the teaching and guidance of your parents and the people who instill great values in you.

If you fall victim to peer pressure, you are exposing yourself to drugs, alcohol, sex and all the other activities you are not ready for as a pre-teen or teen.

The earlier you start to be selective with whom you associate with and being strong with your morals and values, it helps you to resist peer pressure more.

One of the first things you need to do is to let your no be no and stand strongly by it even if you are teased, bullied and treated with disdain.

You should feel comfortable in saying no to do the wrong things. Keep the conversation going with your supportive loved ones and well-wishers.

They will help you through this period. The truth is, it can be very lonely for you when you stand for something good and not following the crowd.

The more you say no, the more you will get accustomed to saying no. You will even empower other pre-teens and teens to start standing up for the right things.

Start thinking about how you will deal with peer pressure before you are even exposed to it.

Talk with your parents, your guidance counsellors, your mentors and people in authority who you trust to talk to on these issues.

Those persons will help you to plan how to deal with peer pressure when you are exposed to it. This gives you confidence and empowers you to do what's right for you.

I cannot deny the fact that your peers have great influence on you, but being prepared to deal with it is a great way of standing up for what you believe in.

You might be at the age where your parents allow you to go to a party or other fun activity with your friends.

Be aware that those are the times when you are away from authority and you become more vulnerable. Be mindful of this!

However, if you are being pressured and you

say no once or twice and you are experiencing more pressure, find a way to contact your parents or other responsible adults.

Getting away from the situation is a way of resisting it, so find a way to leave.

Another way to resist peer pressure is to hang out with friends who share your beliefs and values.

Those peers who talk constantly about their future. This will save you from falling prey to peer pressure.

Remember, you possess the strength to stand up for what you believe in. You don't need to be a part of the crowd. You will be glad you did in the long run. Resist Peer pressure.

CHAPTER 5.4
CHALLENGE YOURSELF

Challenge yourself to do the things you
are uncomfortable doing. That is what
brings growth.

Why put a limit on yourself when you can be and do anything you want to? You have great potential and the earlier you recognize it, the sooner you will start challenging yourself to do great things.

The first thing you can start doing is challenging yourself to do little things which you are uncomfortable doing or fearful of.

An Example of this is trying to eat something you have always thought was not tasty or by challenging your fear of something like height.

If you are a pre-teen or teen who do not like speaking in public, you could find the courage to speak in front of a familiar audience like your school or church.

You could ask your teacher to allow you to do a presentation in class or during assemble. How cool is that!

You could join those extracurricular activities which allow you to do just that. If you go to church, this is a great place to start speaking to an audience. I do this at my church so I you can do it too.

You could speak during Sunday school or even join the youth choir just to face your fears.

This will help you to get over your limitation and on the path to where your true potential really is.

Challenging yourself to do the things your mind tells you that you are not capable of doing allows you to learn new things.

It builds your confidence so much so that you continue to challenge yourself to do even more. Work on your mindset. The more positive your mind is, the more actions you will take.

An example of this is when I challenged

myself to do something which I have never done before. I built my mom's first blog when I was only 12 years old. I'm sure younger persons might have done it before. But I challenged myself and I did it.

The benefit of that is, she saved money and it definitely boosted my confidence. I really felt accomplished.

After doing it, I thought to myself that it wasn't even that difficult as I thought it would have been. The point I'm making is, you can do anything you want to, you just need to challenge yourself and have no excuse not to get it done.

Why put a limit on what you can do when you can be much more than you think you can be. Make today be the day you challenge yourself to be more than the ordinary.

On the following page, make a list of at least five things you can challenge yourself to start doing. Start thinking about how you will do the first one.

Your Task:

Make a list of at least five things you can challenge yourself to start doing. Start thinking about how you will do the first one.

Cons #	Things you can challenge yourself to do
1	
2	
3	
4	
5	

CHAPTER 5.5
REALISTIC GOAL-SETTING IS THE
FOUNDATION FOR SUCCESS

---

*Setting realistic goals is an indication
that you are serious about achieving
them.*

Setting goals is so very important. You might be saying that you don't have goals to set because you are so young.

You are so wrong. We have lots of goals to achieve even as a pre-teen or teen and when you write them down and be focused on them, you are setting up yourself for success.

Some of our immediate or short-term goals could be to get A's in all the subjects for the upcoming exams; it could be to graduate from college or university or to start a business.

Whatever it is for you, make sure you have

them written down and a pathway to get you to accomplish them.

You see how many I managed to outline so far. Yes, we do have goals and the sooner we acknowledge and start writing them down the more serious we will be of achieving them.

You have no excuse not to set your realistic goals and make sure they are written down. You have so many options due to technology. You can use your computer, phone or the good old diary. So, whatever it is you want to use to do this, just go ahead.

The important thing is that no matter where you write down your goals, providing you're working to achieve them, you will certainly do.

I am encouraging you today to start thinking about your goals and make sure you write them down. Talk to your parents, teachers and mentors and they will help you with this.

Let no excuses prevent you from doing this. Your future is dependent on it.

Your Task:

Make a list of at least 5 short term goals and 5 long term goals you want to achieve

Cons #	5 Short Term Goals	5 Long Term Goals
1		
2		
3		
4		
5		

SECTION 3

PARENTS YOUR CHILDREN WANT YOU TO BE PARENT FIRST

As I observed my own parents and how they function as parents, it reminds me that no one is perfect. The moment parents fail to love, communicate and show respect to their children, they are giving them excuse to get it outside the home.

This is why you and your parents must have an ongoing open communication to foster a loving, trusting and nurturing relationship.

CHAPTER 6

YOU ARE THE PARENT

CHAPTER 6.1
BE THE PARENT YOUR CHILD
WANTS YOU TO BE

You are your child's first role model.
Be the parent they can emulate.

The persons children model first are their parents. As they grow older, they begin to model their peers.

As parents, you have to make great effort to set a solid foundation for your children. In doing this, effective parenting is needed.

As children, we want you to be the kind of parents we can model. Not the parents we don't want to see turn up at schools representing us; neither do we want parents who do not have good morals and values which we can emulate. Your children want this, as it will help them to be great men and women of tomorrow.

The truth is, your behavior can be embarrassing for your children. Yes, children should be proud of who their parents are.

However, you have a responsibility as parents to portray yourself in such a way that your children want to be like you.

Your children want you to live by good morals and values and in turn teach it to them. You should demonstrate to your children the importance of living your life by guided principles. When you live by them and teach them to your children actually see them in you every day.

This is encouraging for your children, as you are living what you want them to model.

Another very important part of being effective parents is to teach your preteen and teenage children about those developmental challenges they will go through and some of the things they will encounter outside of the home.

One of the most likely ones is bullying. Don't allow them to get that information from their peers first. That's definitely not good for your children.

Why? Because those topics must be taught in stages and I can promise you that the way they'll hear it from their peers and nefarious individuals is not the correct way.

Based on what I've heard from some of my peers, I know that not all of you parents are able to talk to your children about those topics due to various reasons.

If this is you, make sure you get the appropriate individual who is capable of providing your children with the relevant information. Your children must have those talks.

You want to do this to help to prepare your children for the world, remembering that they will not be around you all the time.

Your children must be able to function outside of the home.

CHAPTER 6.2
HAVE OPEN COMMUNICATION
WITH YOUR CHILDREN

---

*Create an open communication with
your child to foster a trusting and
nurturing relationship.*

Many parents think that they know exactly what's happening with their pre-teen and teenage children.

However, so many parents do not have a clue, most times because they are not communicating with their children. Sometimes when they do try to communicate, it's just not effective.

From my limited knowledge but more importantly, from my home, school, church, books I've read and from experts – nothing works without proper communication. And communicating with your children is no different.

Parents, you need to take the time to effectively communicate with your children to constantly initiate discussions. What you are doing is telling your children that you are always available to talk with them about anything.

You are actually fostering an open line of communication with your children. This will prevent your children from looking outside for answers due to a need. They will trust you so much that they will go to you first when they want answers.

Build a trusting relationship with your children. Yes, you want your children to trust you, but you need to also trust your children.

Once you have instilled good values and morals in your children, trust them that they will do the right things even in your absence.

The reality is, you might do your best as parents and yet, your children still go against what was taught to them.

The fact is, your children are human beings, they are not perfect, and they will mess up.

What you need to do as parents is to point out what your child has done wrong and continue to focus on the positives. What you can do is have a discussion with your child and point out the inappropriate behavior.

Focus on what can be done to correct the behavior rather than the behavior itself. Parents remember this too, don't use it against your child constantly. Instead, focus on moving forward and continue to encourage your child.

Parents, you are teaching your child something that cannot be bought. You are teaching them that they will make mistakes and have failures. The more important thing is learning from the mistakes and failures and try not to repeat them.

How much do you affirm your children? They need to be affirmed because it builds them up. Your affirmation builds your children's confidence and self-esteem.

Your children will believe they can be and do whatever they want to. They believe it for it to happen. It's more powerful than you even realize.

It lets them believe in themselves and their potential. When you do this, the negative things people might say to them like teasing and name calling will not affect too much.

Social media is there, and some parents do not allow their children to be on them. So many youths go against this and secretly use social media for the wrong reasons.

We are living in a time where it's almost impossible to get away from social media no matter your age.

With this in mind, what you should do as parents is to take the opportunity to have dialogue about the advantages and disadvantages of using social media.

Having had the discussion about the advantages and disadvantages of social media, you should then provide guidelines for its use.

The fact is your preteen and teenage children are born in a technological advanced era and if you don't allow them to use social media, they are going to use it when you are not present.

So, the best thing to do is to encourage the proper use and trust that your children will not use it otherwise.

This is an open appeal to parents. Please have constant dialogue with your children as this fosters a trusting relationship.

Now more than ever, you have to make the effort to do this. Remember, if you don't, others will.

CONCLUSION

With each action step you take, you are getting one step closer to achieving your goals.

Youths, we are the future. We will be the men and women who will head countries, lead large and small organizations, be the entrepreneurs who will make millions, the mentors who others will be inspired by and even mothers and fathers to the next generation.

Listen and respect your parents, teacher, mentors and the people in authority. Show respect and regards for your peers' feelings. They might be different, but we are one just the same.

Have a positive mindset and focus your attention on the things you want to achieve. Set your realistic goals and believe in your abilities to make them your reality.

Manage your thoughts and your feelings. When you encounter issues you cannot manage on your own, talk with your parents, guardians or a trusted adult. Always remember this, there's a solution to every problem.

Connect with the right individuals. Those who will be there for you in your times of failures and your successes. Individuals who encourage you to be the best version of yourself.

Take full responsibility for the actions you take. Taking responsibility means you are never in the habit of blaming others for your results.

Parents be the kind of person you want to see in your child. Have constant dialogue with your children. Build that trusting and nurturing relationship.

As I write the final chapter of this book, I charge you to be positive in your thoughts. Dream big, connect with the right individuals and always believe in your ability to achieve anything you want to achieve.

Remember the actions you take today; will determine the success you will have tomorrow.

ABOUT THE AUTHOR
TERRENCE FAGAN JR.

Terrence Fagan Jr. is a 15-year-old youth mentor. He's the founder and host of Youth Empowerment Podcast. A show which inspires, empowers and give business ideas to youths through captivating real-life stories of youths who are experiencing success and experts from varying industries. His show is aired on Apple Podcast (iTunes), Google Play Music, Spotify and Stitcher Radio. Terrence is an online entrepreneur.

Terrence is simultaneously enrolled in college and high school. By the time he graduates high school, he'll also graduate from college with an Associate of Science degree in Computer Programming.

He is the author of numerous journals which are currently sold on Amazon. They are My Daily Action Planner; My Thankfulness & Gratitude Journal and The Prayer Journal.

Terrence is a member of his school's track and field team. He's a fitness fanatic who enjoys working out.

Terrence is on a mission to inspire and empower his peers to take the right actions today to ensure they have the success they want for tomorrow.

To support Terrence on his mission of youth empowerment via his show, Youth Empowerment Podcast, visit **www.YouthEmpowermentPodcast.com** go to the subscribe page to subscribe; download and give a 5 start rating and review. Connect with Terrence on social media **@TerrenceFaganJr.** and **@YouthEmpowermentPodcast.**

To get free youth mentorship, simple join his new Facebook group "Youth Empowered For Success". To contact Terrence for Speaking Engagements, Interviews and/or Youth Mentorship go to **www.YouthEmpowermentPodcast.com** or email **Terrence@YouthEmpowermentPodcast.com**

MY JOURNALS

Get it on Amazon or my website at
www.YouthEmpowermentPodcast.com

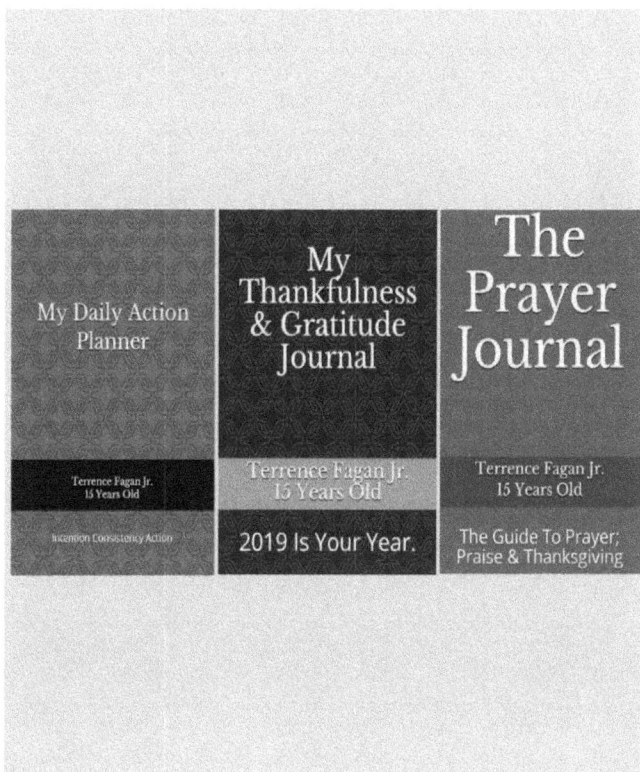

Look out for the 2nd in the series of **Youths Empowered For Success** coming soon.

Terrence Fagan Jr.

www.ingramcontent.com/pod-product-compliance
Lightning Source LLC
Chambersburg PA
CBHW072352090426
42741CB00012B/3020